USBORNE

BOOK OF THE BRAIN AND HOW IT WORKS

Dr. Betina Ip
(Neuroscientist, University of Oxford)

Illustrated by Mia Nilsson

Edited by Alex Frith
Designed by Melissa Gandhi

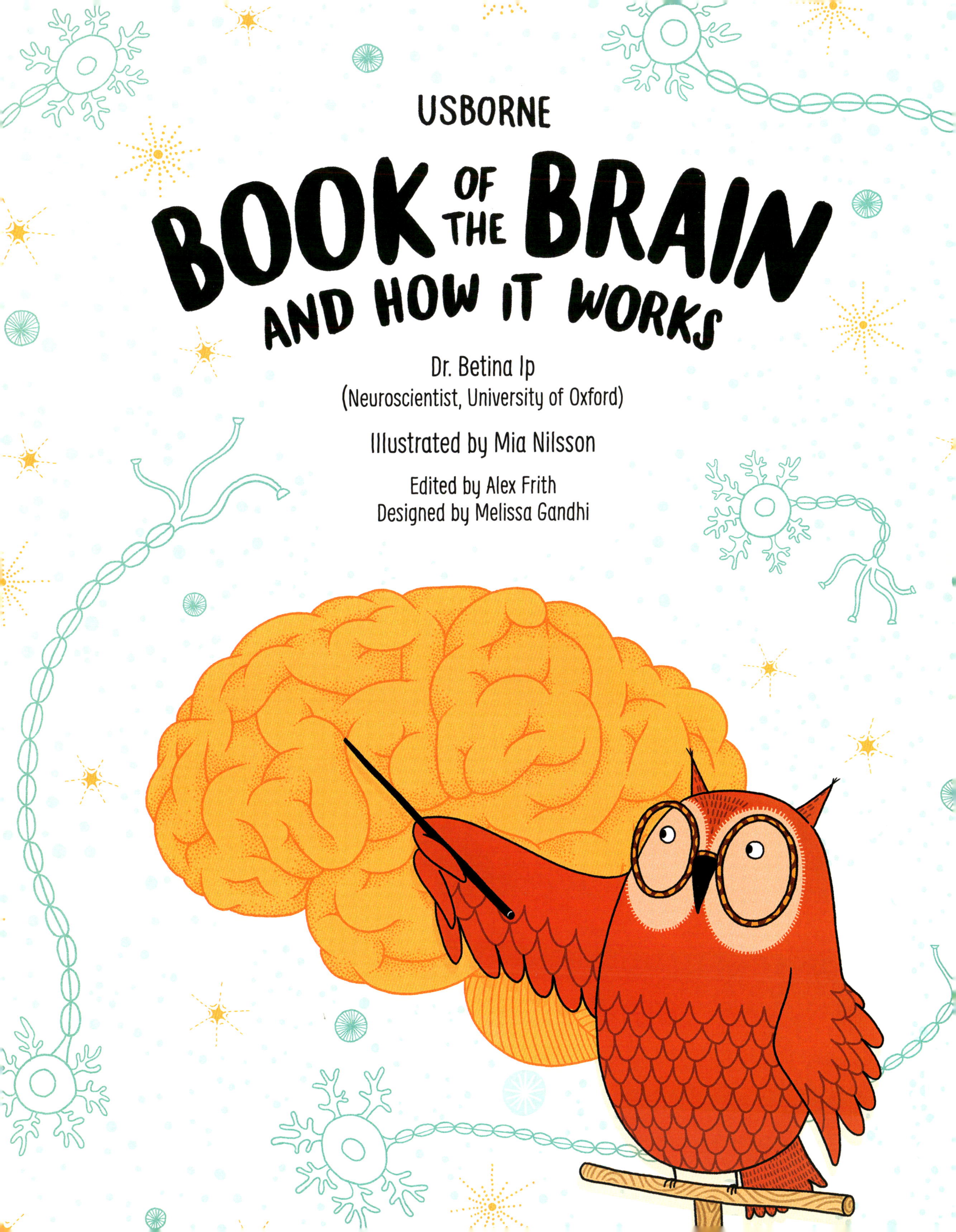

Have you ever wondered how your brain works? How does it learn new skills, such as how to ride a bicycle?
I'm getting really good at riding my bike. I don't even have to think about how to do it, I can just *do* it! I wonder how?

I love daydreaming...
...just letting my thoughts wander through my head.
I wonder where those thoughts come from?
Perhaps I can help! You see, it's all to do with your BRAIN. And I happen to be a brain scientist.
Come with me and I'll show you what I know about how your brain works.
Where are we going?
We're going to step inside your head.
It'll be an adventure!

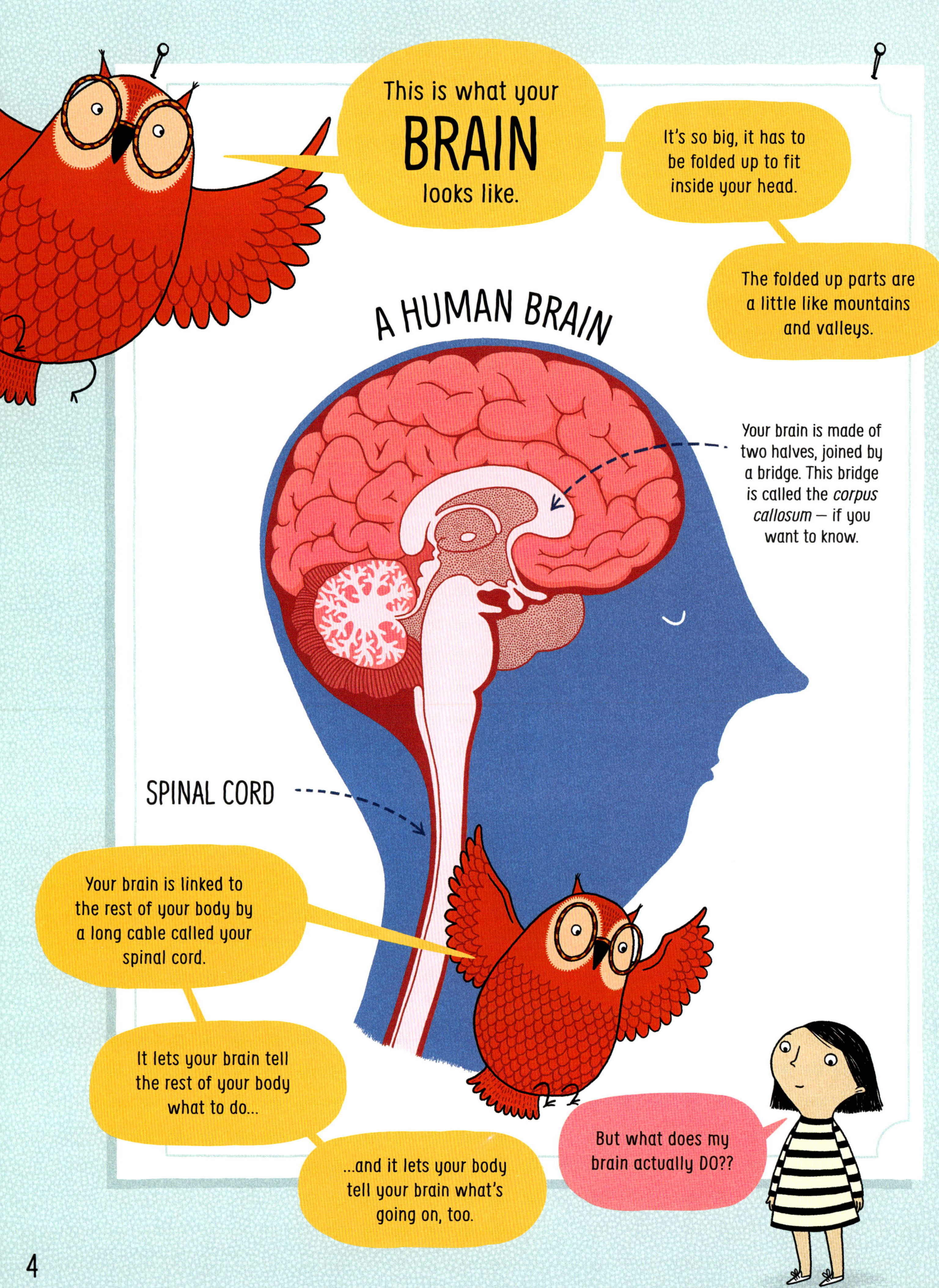
This is what your BRAIN looks like.
It's so big, it has to be folded up to fit inside your head.
The folded up parts are a little like mountains and valleys.
A HUMAN BRAIN
Your brain is made of two halves, joined by a bridge. This bridge is called the *corpus callosum* – if you want to know.
SPINAL CORD
Your brain is linked to the rest of your body by a long cable called your spinal cord.
It lets your brain tell the rest of your body what to do...
...and it lets your body tell your brain what's going on, too.
But what does my brain actually DO??

Your brain does so many wonderful things! Imagine your brain is a city, filled with working parts called BRAIN CELLS.
The city can be divided into five major districts.
There are places to play, places to sing and dance, places to work – everything a person does.
All those places are connected to each other. In fact, your brain cells can talk to each other, no matter how far apart they are.
Here are just a tiny number of the things your brain cells help you to do.
TOUCHING AND FEELING
WHERE?
WHICH?
LATER
NOW
LEFT
RIGHT
RING RING
BANG
BEEEP
ZOOM
WOOF WOOF
LEFT?
RIGHT?
MAKING DECISIONS
WOOF
RING
BEEEP
HEARING
LEARNING SKILLS
SEEING
Wow! There's so much going on! How is it possible?
Brain cells – and the CONNECTIONS between them – are the secret behind everything your brain does.
Your brain is made of thousands and millions and *billions* of these cells. Turn the page to meet some...

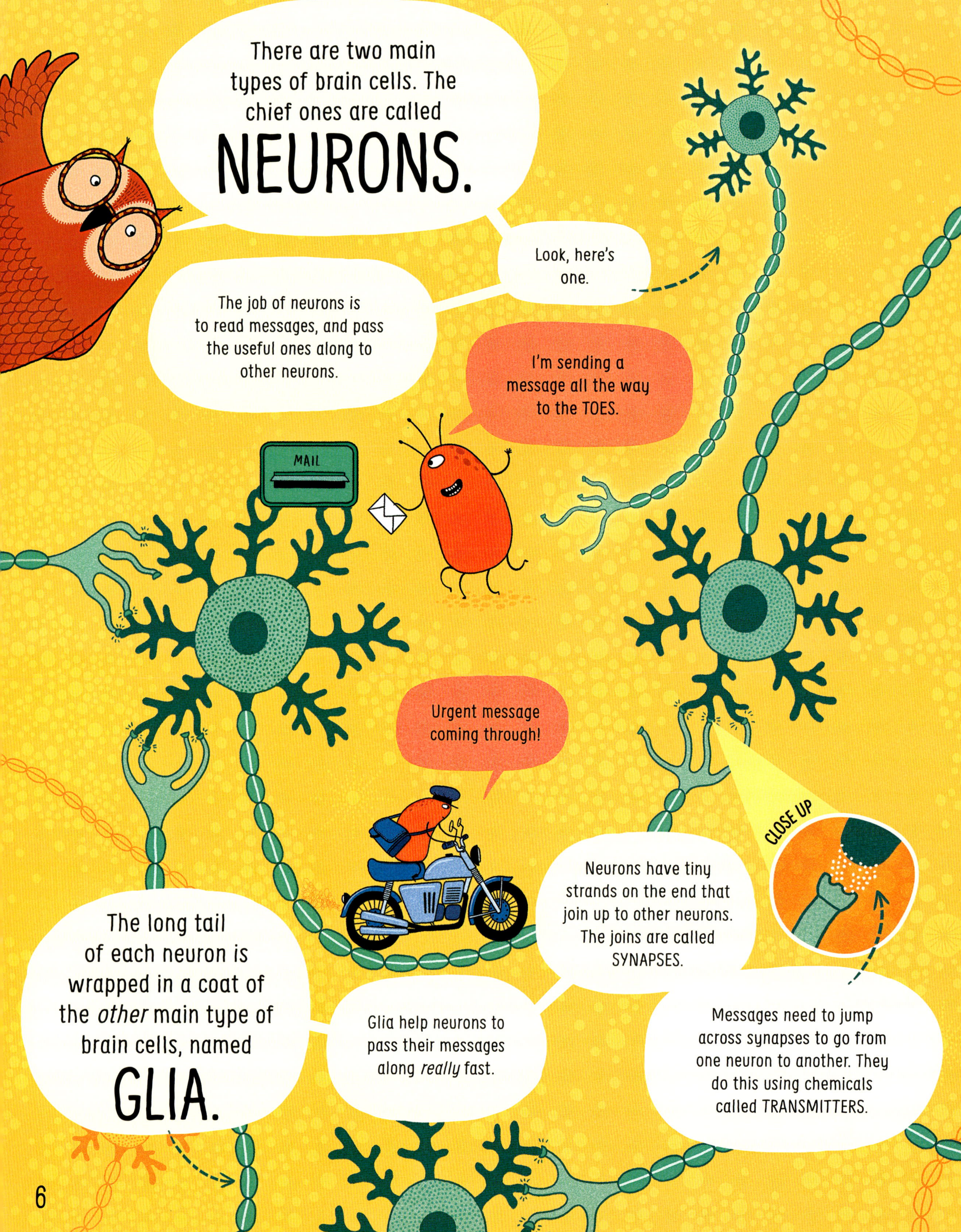
There are two main types of brain cells. The chief ones are called
NEURONS.
Look, here's one.
The job of neurons is to read messages, and pass the useful ones along to other neurons.
I'm sending a message all the way to the TOES.
MAIL
Urgent message coming through!
CLOSE UP
Neurons have tiny strands on the end that join up to other neurons. The joins are called SYNAPSES.
The long tail of each neuron is wrapped in a coat of the *other* main type of brain cells, named
GLIA.
Glia help neurons to pass their messages along *really* fast.
Messages need to jump across synapses to go from one neuron to another. They do this using chemicals called TRANSMITTERS.

MAIL
This message has zoomed along a chain of neurons that runs all down your spinal cord. It's telling your feet to WIGGLE THE TOES.
So every time I use my brain, I'm actually sending letters?
Yes, in a way!
And it's not just a one-way street. Neurons also carry messages *back* to your brain. For example, they collect messages from your eyes, nose, ears, tongue and skin – your senses.
SENSES AT WORK
I'm touching something sticky!
I can taste something sweet!
Listen! I can hear a wrapper crinkling!
I can smell something good to eat!
Look! A chocolate treat!
I can read all these messages because of ELECTRICITY...
...turn the page to find out how this works.

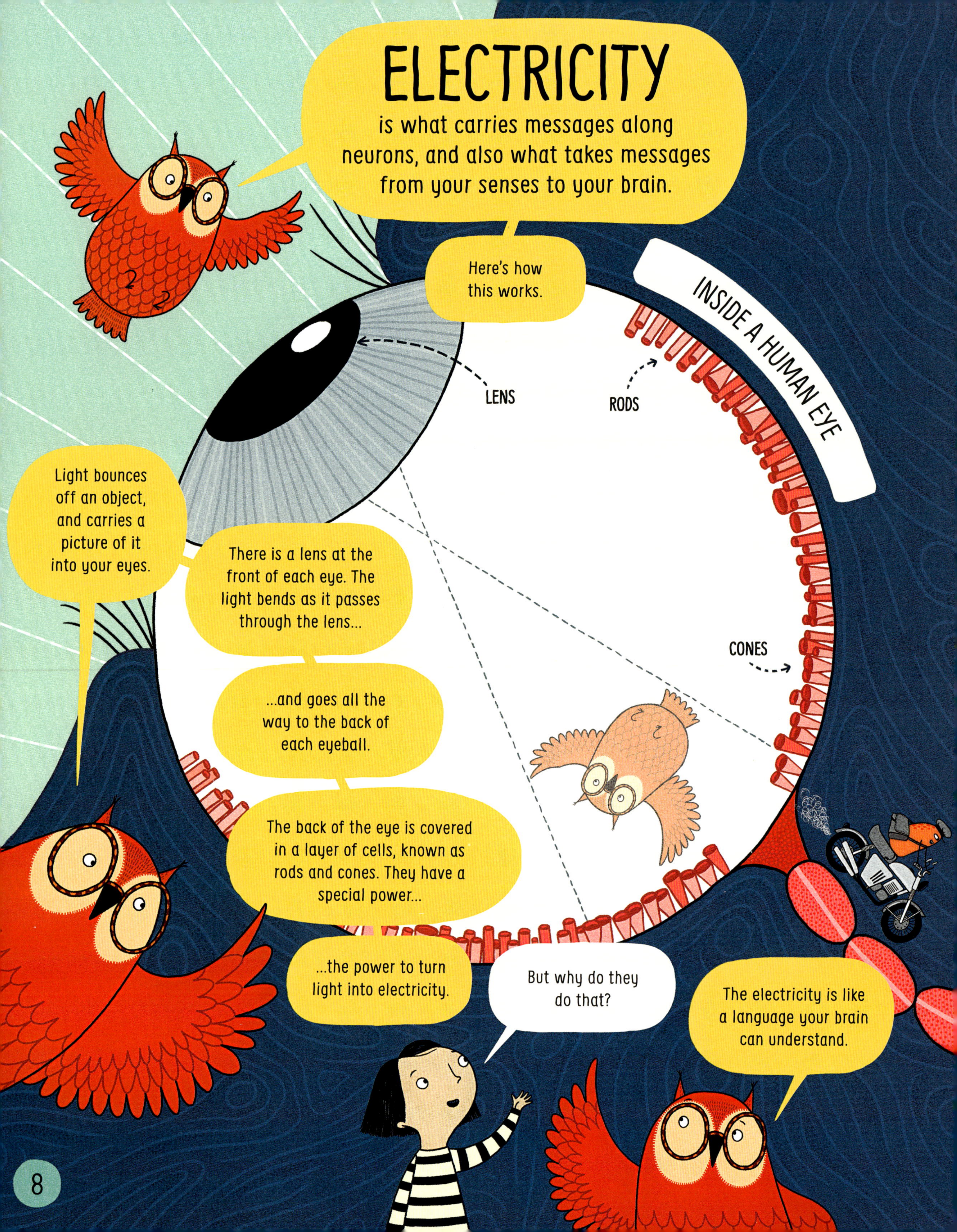
ELECTRICITY
is what carries messages along neurons, and also what takes messages from your senses to your brain.
Here's how this works.
INSIDE A HUMAN EYE
LENS
RODS
CONES
Light bounces off an object, and carries a picture of it into your eyes.
There is a lens at the front of each eye. The light bends as it passes through the lens...
...and goes all the way to the back of each eyeball.
The back of the eye is covered in a layer of cells, known as rods and cones. They have a special power...
...the power to turn light into electricity.
But why do they do that?
The electricity is like a language your brain can understand.

CONES
help see in daytime.

RODS
help see at night.

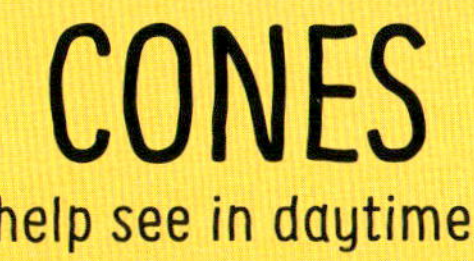

HOW RODS & CONES WORK

Cone cells can pick out all sorts of details – and colours – in bright daylight.

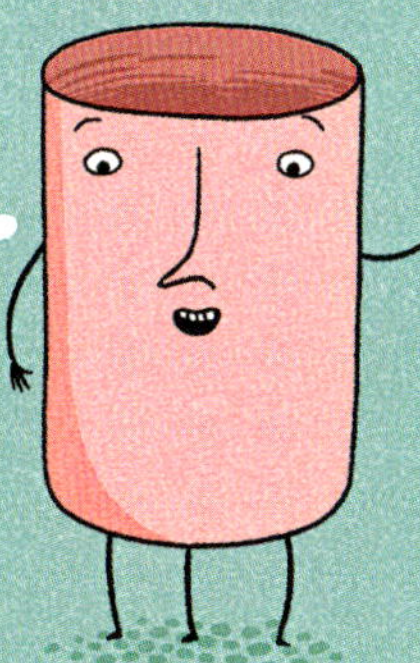

At night, it's too dark for cones. But rod cells collect information even in dim light.

At the end of each rod and cone, parts called TRANSDUCERS gather all the information...

...and transform it into ELECTRIC MESSAGES that your neurons can understand.

Each message is carried all the way to your brain, where neurons are waiting to read the messages.

Electric message coming through!

Electric message coming through!

Messages travel from your eyes to your brain. Turn the page to find out what happens NEXT.

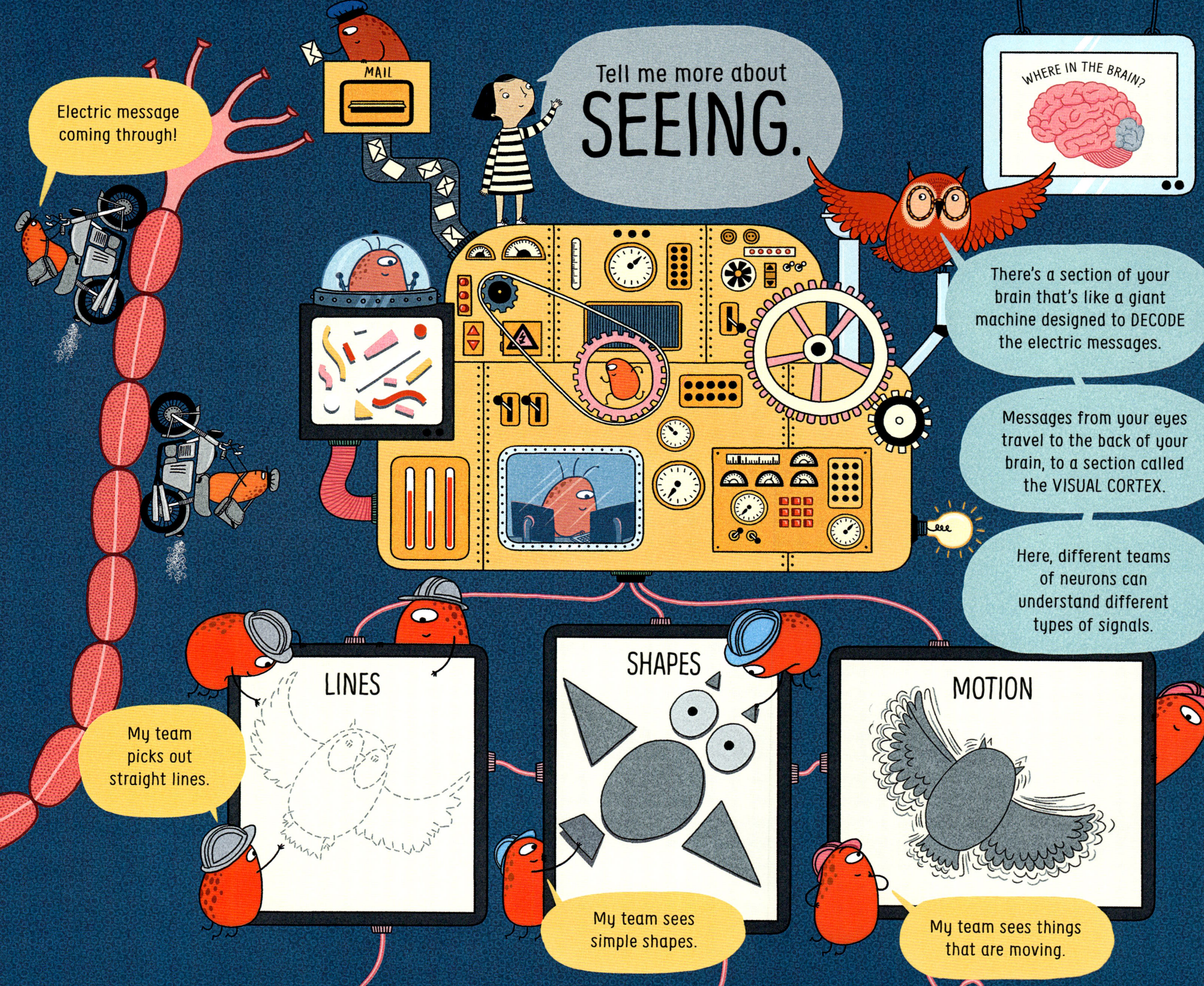
Tell me more about
SEEING.
Electric message coming through!
MAIL
WHERE IN THE BRAIN?
There's a section of your brain that's like a giant machine designed to DECODE the electric messages.
Messages from your eyes travel to the back of your brain, to a section called the VISUAL CORTEX.
Here, different teams of neurons can understand different types of signals.
LINES
SHAPES
MOTION
My team picks out straight lines.
My team sees simple shapes.
My team sees things that are moving.

POSITION
COLOUR
DEPTH
My team sees where an object is, and how parts of it fit together.
My team sees shades and colours.
My team sees three-dimensional objects.
THE WHOLE PICTURE
In other places in your brain, different teams of neurons put the parts together so you can recognize it as a WHOLE THING.
I can see it now – it's a picture of YOU.
Yes. And it's amazing how much of your brain you've used just to give the picture a name.
Let's go and see where some of *THAT* happens – in your brain's MEMORY STORE...

This is your
MEMORY STORE.
It holds memories of who you are, and what you've been doing.
In fact, even the things you are seeing and hearing RIGHT NOW are being kept in a place known as your SHORT-TERM memory.
Your short-term store isn't very big. You can only keep things in here for less than a minute.
SHORT-TERM MEMORIES
Short-term memory coming through!
It helps you do jobs such as remembering a recipe while you're baking.
WHEN I WAS LITTLE
SPECIAL OCCASIONS
But what's in these really BIG boxes?
LONG-TERM MEMORIES
This is your LONG-TERM memory store. The boxes have to hold memories from almost your entire life.
SNAP!
Let's create a new memory! Open up this present...
AAARGH!
We'll take this moment and store some pieces of it in your memory.
We'll remember one piece especially well – the part where you got *scared*.

SHORT-TERM MEMORIES
Most of your recent memories simply disappear, if you don't think about them again.
I want to look in here!
That one's full of memories you think about a lot. Your neurons are really good at finding it quickly.
CHRISTMAS
MY BEST EVER DAYS
BIRTHDAYS
ALL ABOUT ME
HOW TO RIDE A BICYCLE
What about these boxes? They're all ghostly and faint.
NAMES
HOW TO TALK
These hold UNCONSCIOUS memories. That means things you can remember without even thinking about them.
SWIMMING
Would you like to look in this box?
UNCONSCIOUS MEMORIES
FACES
Hmm. I'm not sure why, but I don't like the look of that box.
This is your unconscious memory at work. Even though you don't recognize the box...
...your brain remembers that it had something scary in it.

Speaking of scary things, let's visit the hall of **EMOTIONS.**

Emotions help you react to things that go on in the world around you.

When you're very young, your brain learns to recognize emotions in the people around you.

Scientists say there are SIX BASIC EMOTIONS. Each one has its own face.

SURPRISE

ANGER

HAPPINESS

I like the yellow face best! It makes me smile.

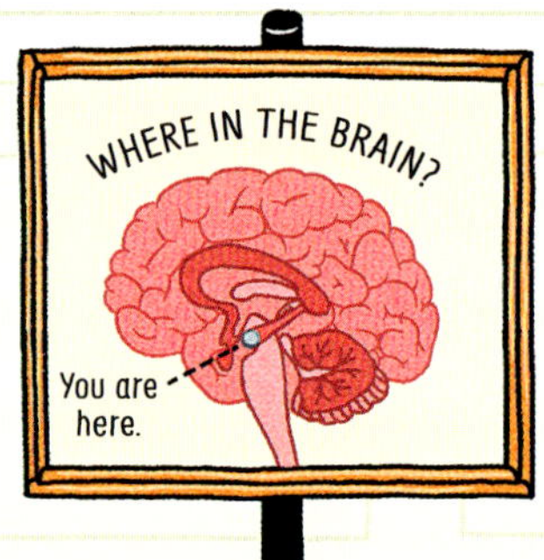

That's because your brain likes to copy other people.

When you see someone smiling, it can make *you* smile, and might even make you feel happier.

People all over the world show emotions in the same way. It means we can recognize each other's emotions even when we're with people who speak different languages.
FEAR
DISGUST
SADNESS
SPIDER! AAAARGH!
I hate feeling scared.
It's not nice, but it's very *useful*. When you're scared, your brain gets your body ready to run away, or fight.
I'm tired. Is that an emotion?
No – it's your brain's way of telling you that it needs to sleep. Come and find out more...

YAAAWN! I'm SLEEPY.
WHERE IN THE BRAIN?
You are here.
Did you know, while you sleep, your brain is still hard at work?
For a start, there are sensors checking the world around you.
When it gets dark, these sensors tell your brain to start a sleep cycle...
Your brain's sleep controls can pump out chemicals called HORMONES that send messages to all parts of your body.
SLEEP CYCLE MACHINE
STAGE 1
LIGHT SLEEP
Eyes move a little
Z Z Z Z
STAGE 2
DEEP SLEEP
Eyes stop moving
STAGE 3
DEEPER SLEEP
STAGE 4
DREAM SLEEP
Eyes move very fast
END OF CYCLE
OPTION 1
OPTION 2
Option 1: wake up
Option 2: back to Stage 1
Sleep is good for many reasons, such as keeping your brain TIDY, helping you LEARN, letting your muscles SHUT DOWN for a bit, and...
...it's the time when you can have DREAMS.

MUSCLE SHUTDOWN
During dream sleep, your brain shuts down connections to your muscles, so you don't act out your dreams.
DREAMING
Dreaming is a big part of being asleep, even if you don't remember your dreams. But no one knows why dreams happen, and if they mean anything.
You only remember a dream if you happen to wake up in the middle of one.
TIDYING UP
While you sleep, your brain can tidy up the spaces between neurons.
LEARNING
Sleeping brains have time to think about all the new things they've discovered that day.
A IS FOR APPLE
French = pomme
German = apfel
Japanese = ringo
RECORDER PRACTICE
Twinkle twinkle little star
= c c g g a a g
Teams of neurons re-play memories while you sleep. This helps you learn.
One of the things your sleeping brain is busy doing is something that happens when you're awake, too. Turn the page to see...

WHERE IN THE BRAIN?
You are here.
Deep in your brain there are neurons busy simply keeping your
BODY ALIVE.
Most of the time, your body is safe and calm.
HEARTBEAT
BEAT!
BEAT!
Teams of neurons remind your heart to beat and your lungs to breathe.
All quiet.
BREATHING
HUFF!
PUFF!
Some neurons run up and down your spinal cord carrying messages to the different teams.
When you're resting, it's a good time to digest the food in your tummy.
Some neurons are on the look out to check the world around you.
WHAT'S GOING ON AROUND ME?
BURNING FOOD FOR FUEL
What's that..?
All quiet.
There's a spider! Sound the alert!
ROAR!
ROAR!

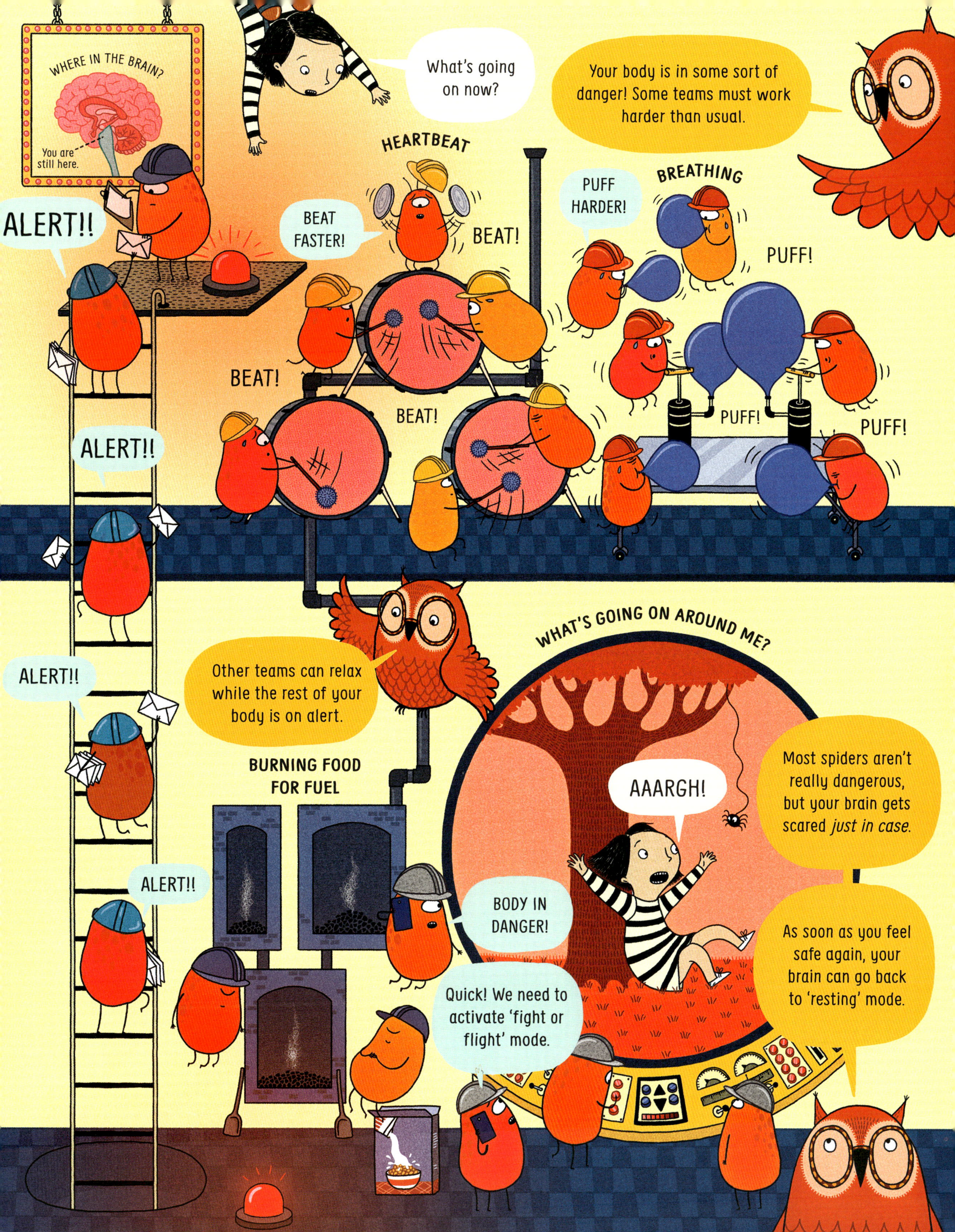
WHERE IN THE BRAIN?
You are still here.
What's going on now?
Your body is in some sort of danger! Some teams must work harder than usual.
HEARTBEAT
BEAT FASTER!
BEAT!
BEAT!
BEAT!
BREATHING
PUFF HARDER!
PUFF!
PUFF!
PUFF!
ALERT!!
ALERT!!
ALERT!!
ALERT!!
Other teams can relax while the rest of your body is on alert.
BURNING FOOD FOR FUEL
WHAT'S GOING ON AROUND ME?
AAARGH!
Most spiders aren't really dangerous, but your brain gets scared *just in case*.
BODY IN DANGER!
Quick! We need to activate 'fight or flight' mode.
As soon as you feel safe again, your brain can go back to 'resting' mode.

It's time to make a DECISION. What would you like to do now?

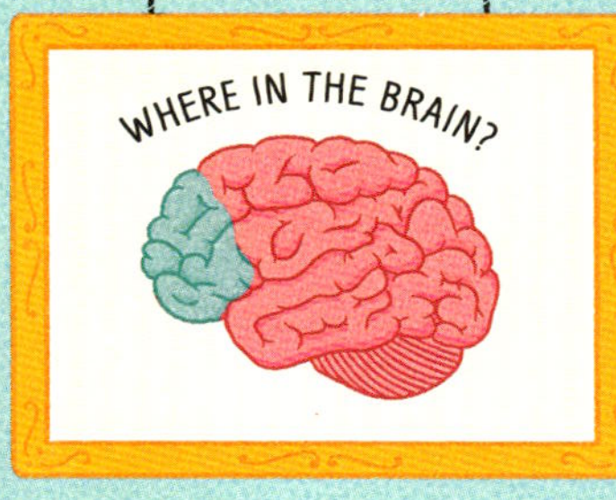

I'm hungry. May I have an ice cream, please?

Yes — but which kind of ice cream would you like? You'll have to make a few more decisions...

Most of the things you do need you to make *choices*. Let's imagine each choice is like a thought bubble that you have to pop.

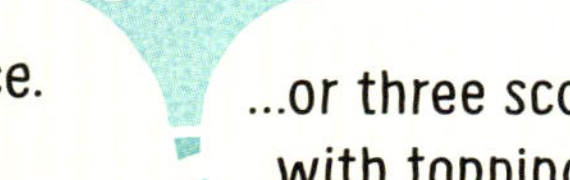

Here's the first bubble. Would you like to go to an ice cream van...

...or to a café?

A short wait, but not many flavours.

A longer wait, but loads and loads of flavours.

The café — good choice!

On to the next choice. Would you like a single scoop of plain ice cream...

...or three scoops with toppings?

NOT TOO EXPENSIVE

VERY EXPENSIVE

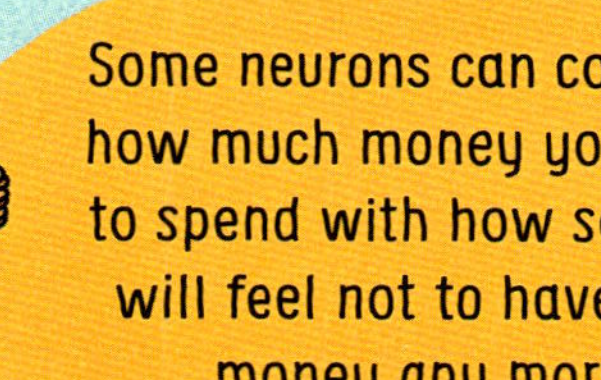

Some of your neurons do the job of deciding how quickly you want this treat.

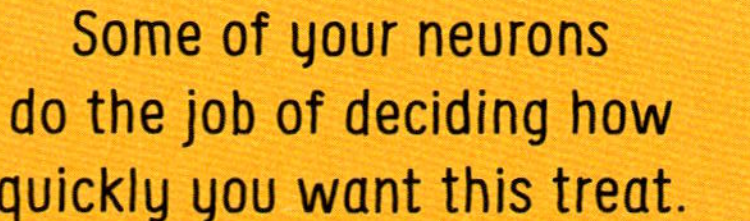

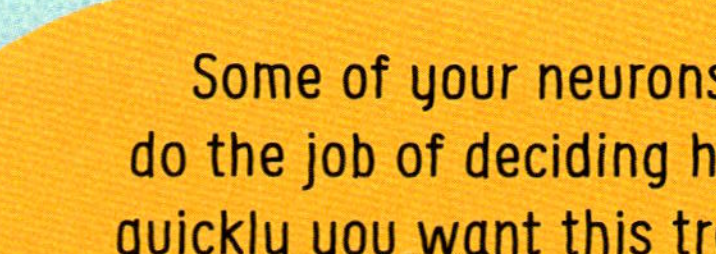

Some neurons can compare how much money you have to spend with how sad you will feel not to have that money any more.

Another decision, and this one's all about LOTS of choice.
Which out of all these flavours would you like?
Sometimes, it's easier to make decisions by thinking about what emotions you're feeling.
Aaargh! There's *too much choice*, I can't take it all in.
Luckily, there are neurons that stop you from overloading with information. They help your brain focus on just a few options.
Yum!
Blurgh! I feel too full now. I wish I'd chosen a smaller treat.
Never mind – bad experiences are actually really important.
They help your brain make better decisions next time. This is a big part of LEARNING...

Welcome to your brain's
LEARNING GARDEN.
This is where you can improve your decision making, and your skills.
The real secret to neurons is how well they are CONNECTED to each other.
It's so tangled in here. Like lots of plants twisted together.
Exactly.
When you're little, your neurons have LOTS and LOTS of connections. It's *really* tangled in your brain!
Learning new things is all about making USEFUL connections stronger, and getting rid of UNHELPFUL ones.
UNTANGLING NEURONS
To make your brain do something, you have to send a message along one branch of neurons.
If it's a helpful branch, your brain will try to remember the route.
✓
If it's an unhelpful branch...
×
...your brain will cut it off, so you don't use it again.

When you use your brain to do anything, you need to send a signal across your tangled branches.
Learning how to do something – whether it's walking, talking or brushing your teeth – is all about finding the best way through.
Practising a skill is a mixture of two things: *cutting away* branches that you don't need...
...and making the branches you *do* need stronger and stronger.
But it's hard to know which branches to cut away. And that means we all make lots of mistakes while we're learning.
I'm not afraid of making mistakes now I know it helps me learn better.

Just like any part of your body, your brain needs
LOOKING AFTER.
There are lots of things you can do to take care of it.
Your brain loves EXERCISE! Jumping, dancing, playing – any kind of moving around – makes your brain send messages around your body that make you feel happy.
Your brain loves FOOD! Especially a balanced diet – any mix of foods that keeps your *body* healthy will also keep your *brain* healthy.
Your brain loves OTHER BRAINS! It's good to spend time with your family, your friends, and to meet new people.
Your brain loves SLEEP! It's not just good for learning. Sleep helps you cope with everyday life more easily, and can stop you from feeling too sad.

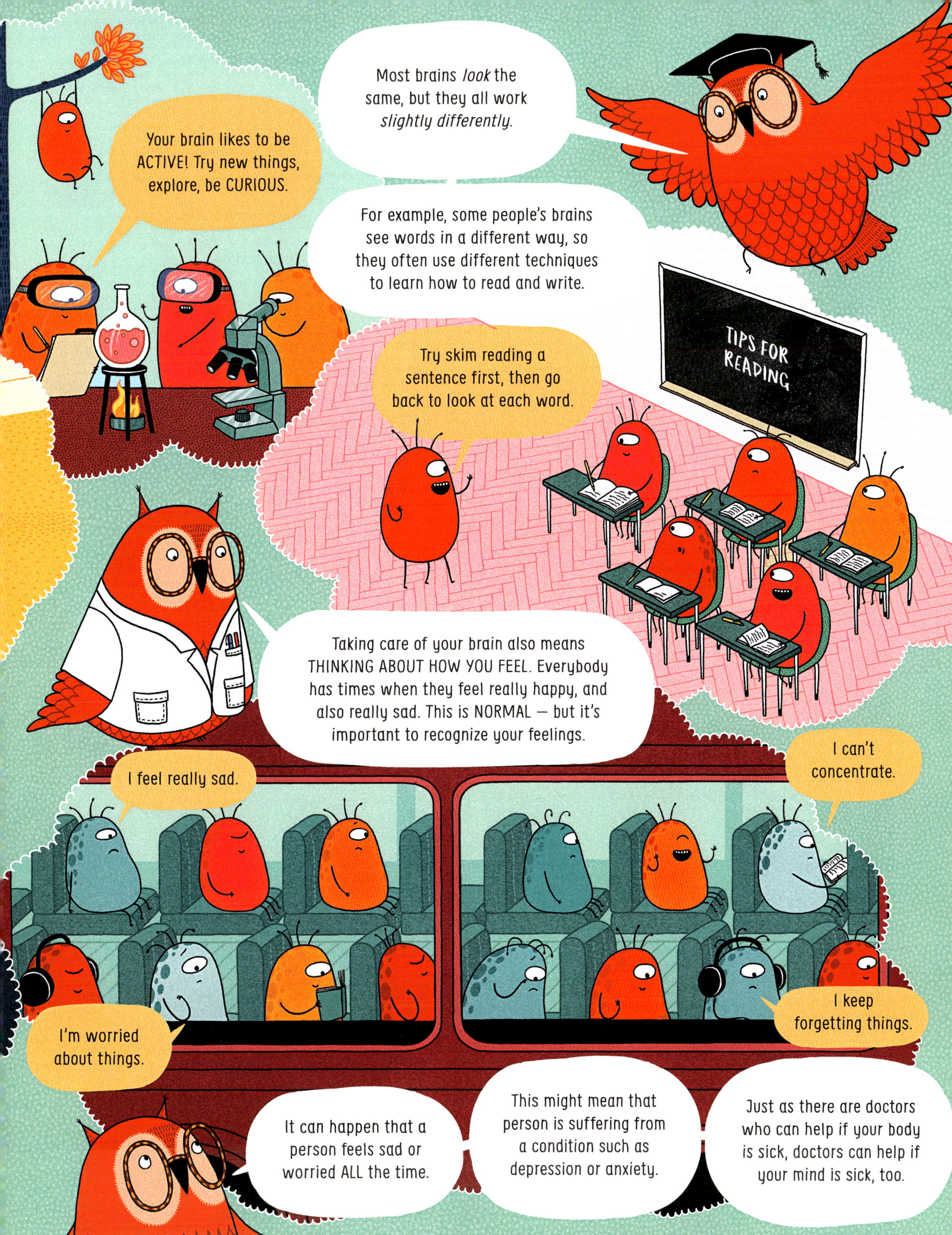
Your brain likes to be ACTIVE! Try new things, explore, be CURIOUS.
Most brains *look* the same, but they all work *slightly differently*.
For example, some people's brains see words in a different way, so they often use different techniques to learn how to read and write.
TIPS FOR READING
Try skim reading a sentence first, then go back to look at each word.
Taking care of your brain also means THINKING ABOUT HOW YOU FEEL. Everybody has times when they feel really happy, and also really sad. This is NORMAL – but it's important to recognize your feelings.
I feel really sad.
I can't concentrate.
I'm worried about things.
I keep forgetting things.
It can happen that a person feels sad or worried ALL the time.
This might mean that person is suffering from a condition such as depression or anxiety.
Just as there are doctors who can help if your body is sick, doctors can help if your mind is sick, too.

I've learned so many amazing things already! But how do we know so much about our brains?
Let me show you. Here we are in my
BRAIN SCIENCE
study. My friends are hard at work.
What's this?
It's a machine called a brain scanner. I'm using it to see what's happening inside this person's brain while she's thinking. She has to stay very still.
This screen shows her brain. The bright parts are where extra blood is flowing. That means the brain is working hard in those parts.
I'm looking at old neurons through a microscope. Some of them are very beautiful.
I'm using a computer to test ideas about how brains work. I want to see if I can make my computer think like a person.

This is our medicine cabinet. Lots of brain problems can be helped by taking the right kinds of medicines, but they have to be tested very carefully.
This is our library. We read lots of science books about brains.
We also love looking at art, and reading stories. Almost everything that people create tells us about what's going on in their brains.
That looks fun! What are they doing?
They're doing an experiment. My friend wants to see what happens when they try to build two different puzzles at the same time.
What do you call people who study brains?
People who study how we think and behave are called PSYCHOLOGISTS.
People who study what brains are made of, and how they work, are called NEUROSCIENTISTS.
Doctors who help people look after their mental health are called PSYCHIATRISTS.
Can I be a neuroscientist, too?
By asking questions about your brain, you already are! All you need to get started is CURIOSITY.
Do you have any more questions?

Are BIG brains CLEVERER?
Do animals have neurons, too?
What about ants – do they have brains?
I HAVE LOTS AND *LOTS* OF QUESTIONS!
What do the FOLDS in my brain do?
Do all neurons look the same?
How did I learn to TALK?
How BIG will my brain get?

Yes.
No.
Yes, ants have simple, tiny brains.
Let me try to give you some
ANSWERS!
They allow all your neurons to fit inside your head.
About the same size as two fists pressed together.
No, they come in many shapes and sizes.
Learning to talk starts with a baby language called BABBLING.
I also have a secret to share with you...
...brain scientists only know a *little* about how brains work. There are so many MORE things to discover. If you become a neuroscientist, perhaps YOU will find out something about brains that nobody ever knew before.

Here are some

BRAIN FACTS

we *DO* know.

By the time you're **born** your brain has **almost all** the neurons it will ever have.

That's why babies have such big heads.

By the time you're **two years old** your brain has nearly as many neurons as there are **stars in the galaxy** – around **80 BILLION!**

Every time you **think** or **remember** or just ***do*** anything, you're using millions of neurons to send messages.

Teenage brains can get **overloaded** with connections between their neurons.

My brain is INCREDIBLE!
By the time you're 25, your grown-up brain has strengthened the best connections, until they shine out like constellations in the night sky.

INDEX

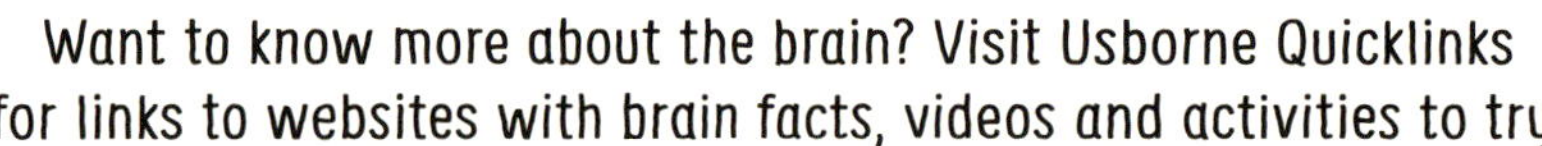

Want to know more about the brain? Visit Usborne Quicklinks for links to websites with brain facts, videos and activities to try.

Go to usborne.com/Quicklinks and type in the keywords "book of the brain". Please read the internet safety guidelines at Usborne Quicklinks. Children should be supervised online.

Brain expert: Professor Holly Bridge,
Nuffield Department of Clinical Neurosciences, University of Oxford

Managing designer: Stephen Moncrieff
With thanks to Mary Cartwright and Jane Chisholm

For Bianca and Yulian, with love

Background photograph on p30-31 © Sripfoto/Dreamstime.com

First published in 2020 by Usborne Publishing Ltd.,
Usborne House, 83-85 Saffron Hill, London EC1N 8RT, England.